How To Use This Book

I am happy to share this second volume of Baha'i themed colouring pages. The purpose of this book is to use it as an added resource for the spiritual education of children.

You are welcome to photocopy as many individual pages as needed. It is my hope that you get many years use out of this book and that children participating in classes enjoy colouring the pictures and reading the Baha'i quotes. I plan to continue putting together more volumes over time and any feedback is most welcome.
Enjoy
Monika

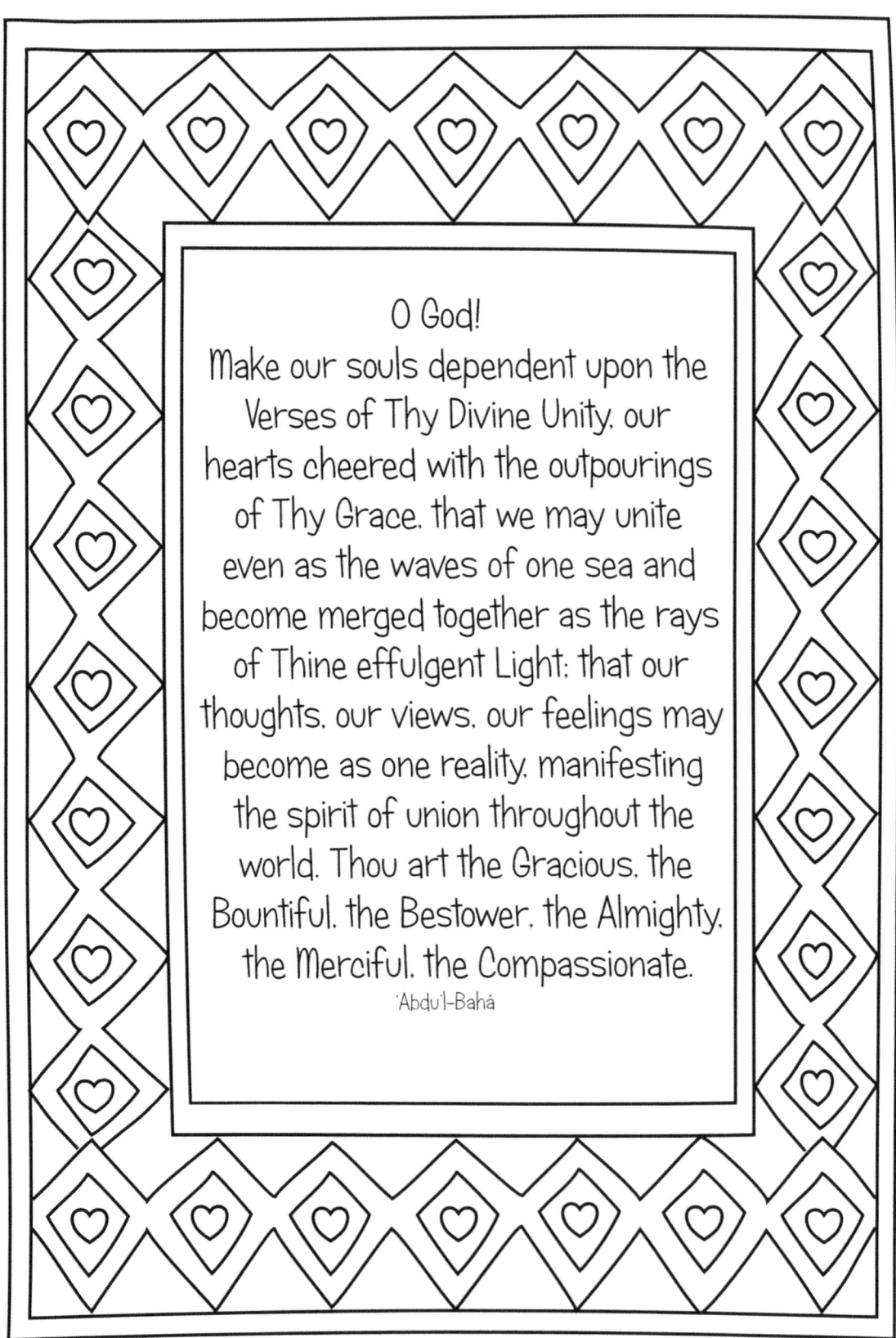

O God!
Make our souls dependent upon the Verses of Thy Divine Unity, our hearts cheered with the outpourings of Thy Grace, that we may unite even as the waves of one sea and become merged together as the rays of Thine effulgent Light; that our thoughts, our views, our feelings may become as one reality, manifesting the spirit of union throughout the world. Thou art the Gracious, the Bountiful, the Bestower, the Almighty, the Merciful, the Compassionate.

‘Abdu'l-Bahá

Turn all your thoughts toward bringing joy to hearts. Beware! Beware! lest ye offend any heart. Assist the world of humanity as much as possible. —'Abdu'l-Bahá

All the virtues which have been deposited and potential in human hearts are being revealed from that Reality as flowers and blossoms from divine gardens. It is a day of joy, a time of happiness, a period of spiritual growth.

'Abdu'l-Bahá

Gather all people beneath the shadow of Thy bounty and cause them to unite in harmony, so that they may become as the rays of one sun, as the waves of one ocean, and as the fruit of one tree.
'Abdu'l-Bahá

Bookmark 1:

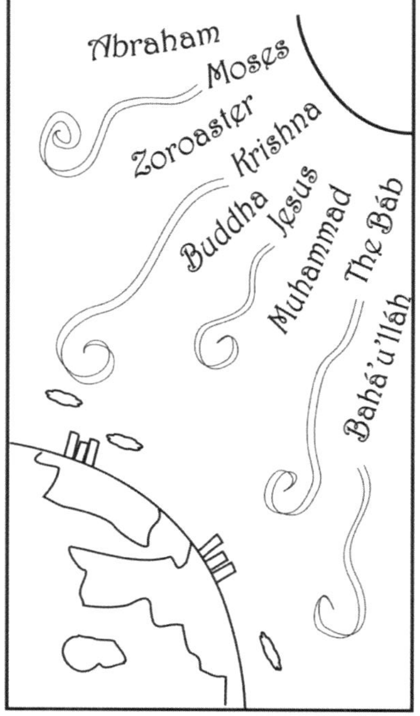

The fruits of the human tree are exquisite, highly desired and dearly cherished. Among them are upright character, virtuous deeds and a goodly utterance.

—Bahá'u'lláh

(Basket of fruits labeled: Gentleness, Excellence, Caring, Humility, Honesty, Courtesy, Tolerance, Kindness, Joy)

Bookmark 2:

What, then, is the mission of the divine Prophets? Their mission is the education and advancement of the world of humanity. They are the real Teachers and Educators, the universal Instructors of mankind.

—'Abdu'l-Bahá

(Names: Abraham, Moses, Zoroaster, Krishna, Buddha, Jesus, Muhammad, The Báb, Bahá'u'lláh)

Bookmark 3:

I am a flower in God's garden.

Bookmark 4:

O people of the world, ye are all the fruit of one tree and the leaves of one branch. Walk with perfect charity, concord, affection, and agreement.

—'Abdu'l-Bahá

"The education and training of children is among the most meritorious acts of humankind..."
Bahá'í Writings

"The education and training of children is among the most meritorious acts of humankind and draweth down the grace and favour of the All-Merciful, for education is the indispensable foundation of all human excellence and alloweth man to work his way to the heights of abiding glory."
Bahá'í Writings

"The education and training of children is among the most meritorious acts of humankind."
Bahá'í Writings

"The education and training of children is among the most meritorious acts of humankind and draweth down the grace and favour of the All-Merciful, for education is the indispensable foundation of all human excellence and alloweth man to work his way to the heights of abiding glory."
Bahá'í Writings

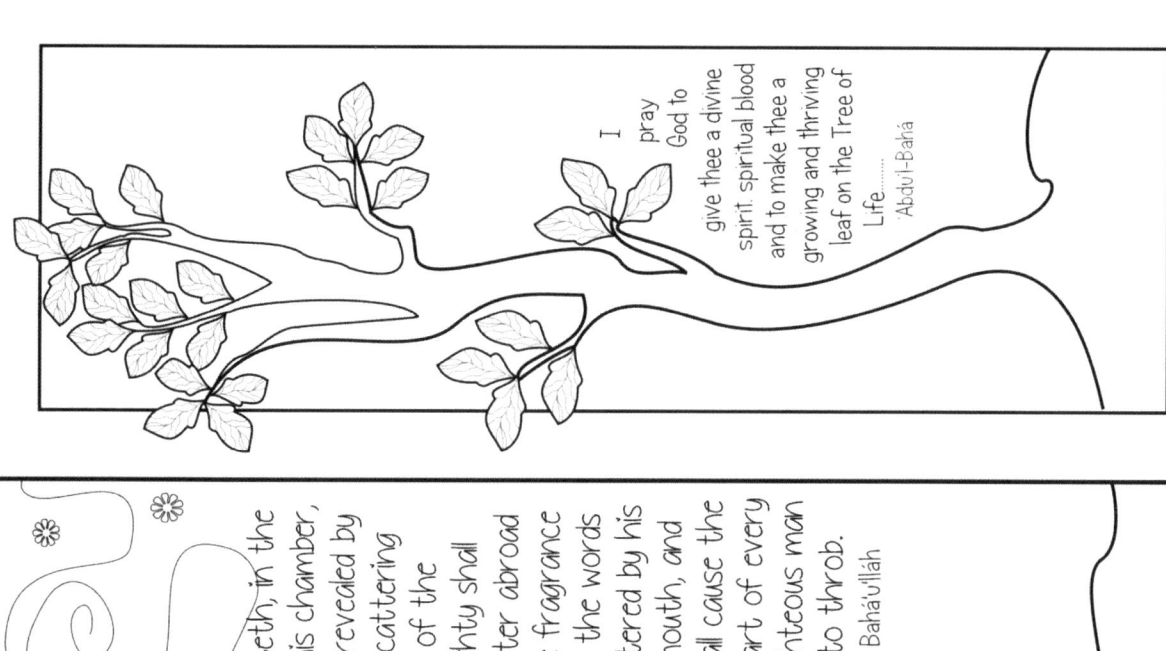

I pray God to give thee a divine spirit, spiritual blood and to make thee a growing and thriving leaf on the Tree of Life........
'Abdu'l-Bahá

Whoso reciteth, in the privacy of his chamber, the verses revealed by God, the scattering angels of the Almighty shall scatter abroad the fragrance of the words uttered by his mouth, and shall cause the heart of every righteous man to throb.
Bahá'u'lláh

Ye are the saplings which the hand of Loving-kindness hath planted in the soil of mercy, and which the showers of bounty have made to flourish.
Bahá'u'lláh

I bear witness, O my God, that Thou hast created me to know Thee and to worship Thee. I testify, at this moment, to my powerlessness and to Thy might, to my poverty and to Thy wealth. There is none other God but Thee, the Help in Peril, the Self-Subsisting.
Bahá'u'lláh

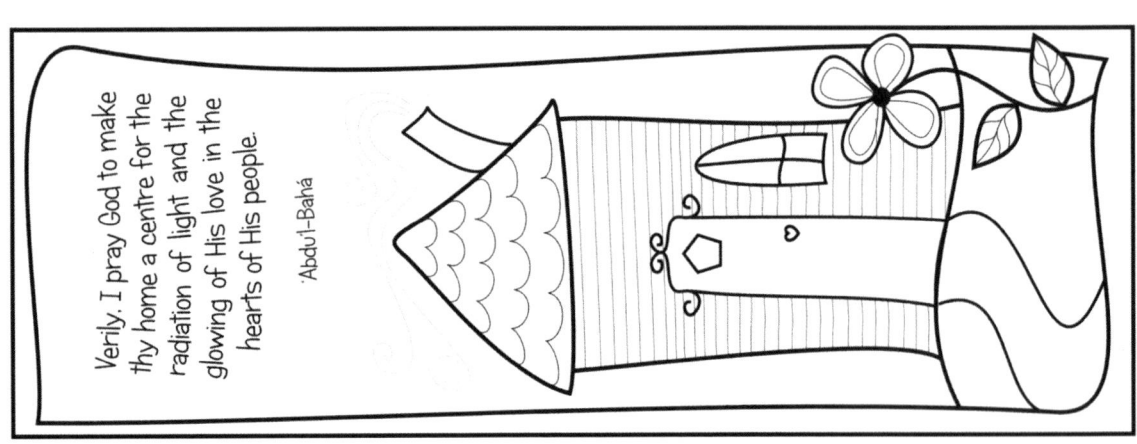

Verily, I pray God to make thy home a centre for the radiation of light and the glowing of His love in the hearts of His people.

'Abdu'l-Bahá

The gentle breezes wafted from the garden of their hearts shall perfume and revive the souls of men, and the revelations of their minds, even as showers, reinvigorate the peoples and nations of the world.

'Abdu'l-Bahá

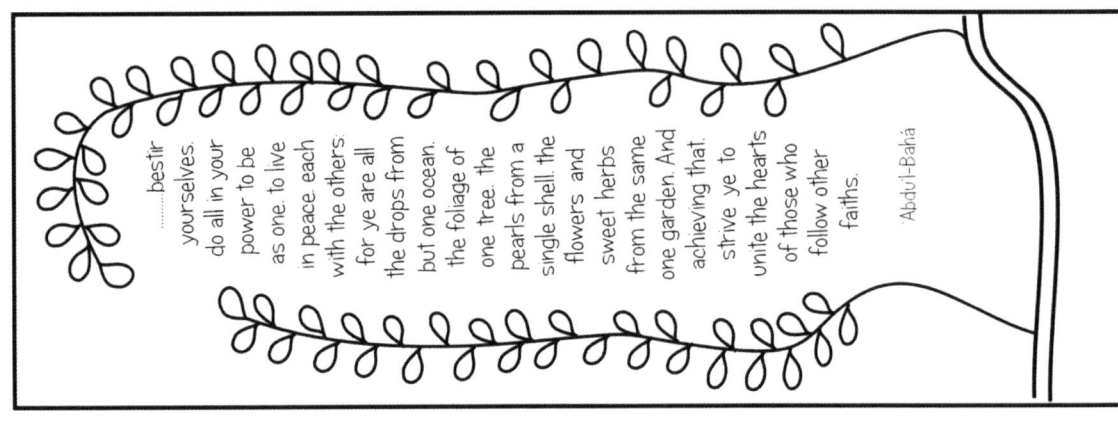

……bestir yourselves, do all in your power to be as one, to live in peace, each with the others: for ye are all the drops from but one ocean, the foliage of one tree, the pearls from a single shell, the flowers and sweet herbs from the same one garden. And achieving that, strive ye to unite the hearts of those who follow other faiths.

'Abdu'l-Bahá

Man is like unto a tree. If he be adorned with fruit, he hath been and will ever be worthy of praise and commendation. Otherwise a fruitless tree is but fit for fire. The fruits of the human tree are exquisite, highly desired and dearly cherished. Among them are upright character, virtuous deeds and a goodly utterance.

Bahá'u'lláh

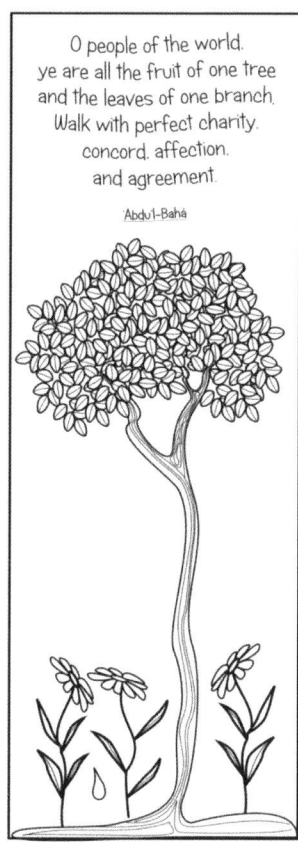

O people of the world, ye are all the fruit of one tree and the leaves of one branch. Walk with perfect charity, concord, affection, and agreement.

'Abdu'l-Bahá

I am a flower in God's garden.

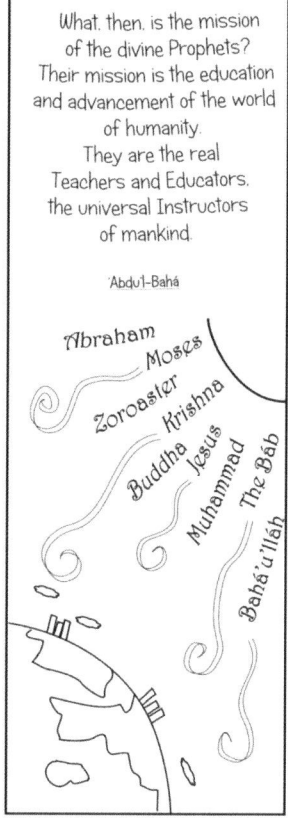

What, then, is the mission of the divine Prophets? Their mission is the education and advancement of the world of humanity. They are the real Teachers and Educators, the universal Instructors of mankind.

'Abdu'l-Bahá

Abraham, Moses, Zoroaster, Krishna, Buddha, Jesus, Muhammad, The Báb, Bahá'u'lláh

The fruits of the human tree are exquisite, highly desired and dearly cherished. Among them are upright character, virtuous deeds and a goodly utterance.

Bahá'u'lláh

Gentleness, Humility, Excellence, Kindness, Honesty, Caring, Joy, Courtesy, Tolerance

"The education and training of children is among the most meritorious acts of humankind and draweth down the grace and favour of the All-Merciful, for education is the indispensable foundation of all human excellence and alloweth man to work his way to the heights of abiding glory."

Bahá'í Writings

"The education and training of children is among the most meritorious acts of humankind..."

Bahá'í Writings

"The education and training of children is among the most meritorious acts of humankind and draweth down the grace and favour of the All-Merciful, for education is the indispensable foundation of all human excellence and alloweth man to work his way to the heights of abiding glory."

Bahá'í Writings

"The education and training of children is among the most meritorious acts of humankind..."

Bahá'í Writings

"... Say: No man can attain his true station except through his justice. No power can exist except through unity. No welfare and no well-being can be attained except through consultation.

Bahá'u'lláh

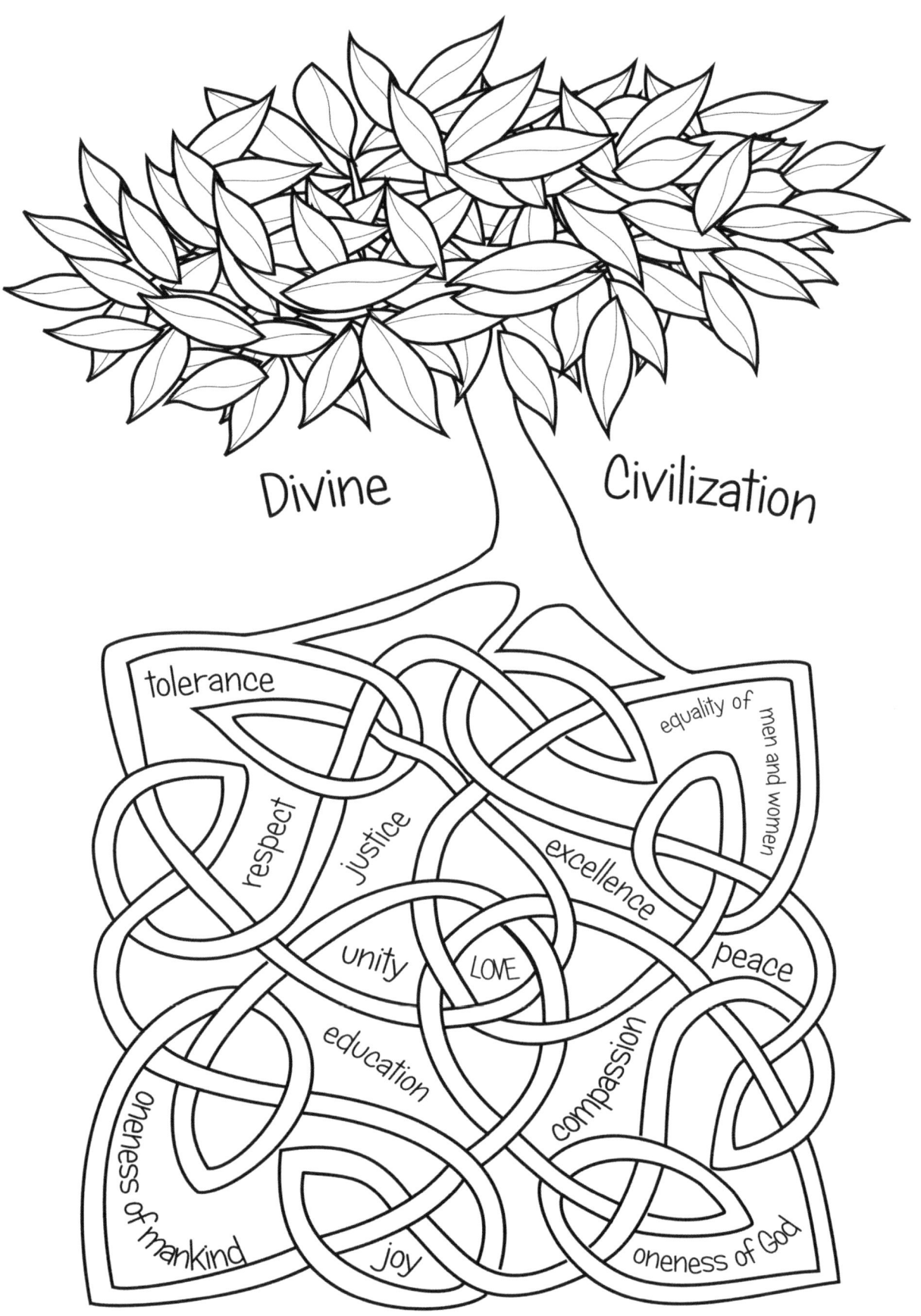

O Lord! Grant Thine infinite bestowals, and let the light of Thy guidance shine. Illumine the eyes, gladden the hearts with abiding joy. Confer a new spirit upon all people and bestow upon them eternal life. Unlock the gates of true understanding and let the light of faith shine resplendent. Gather all people beneath the shadow of Thy bounty and cause them to unite in harmony, so that they may become as the rays of one sun, as the waves of one ocean, and as the fruit of one tree. May they drink from the same fountain. May they be refreshed by the same breeze. May they receive illumination from the same source of light. Thou art the Giver, the Merciful, the Omnipotent. - 'Abdu'l-Bahá

O Lord God!

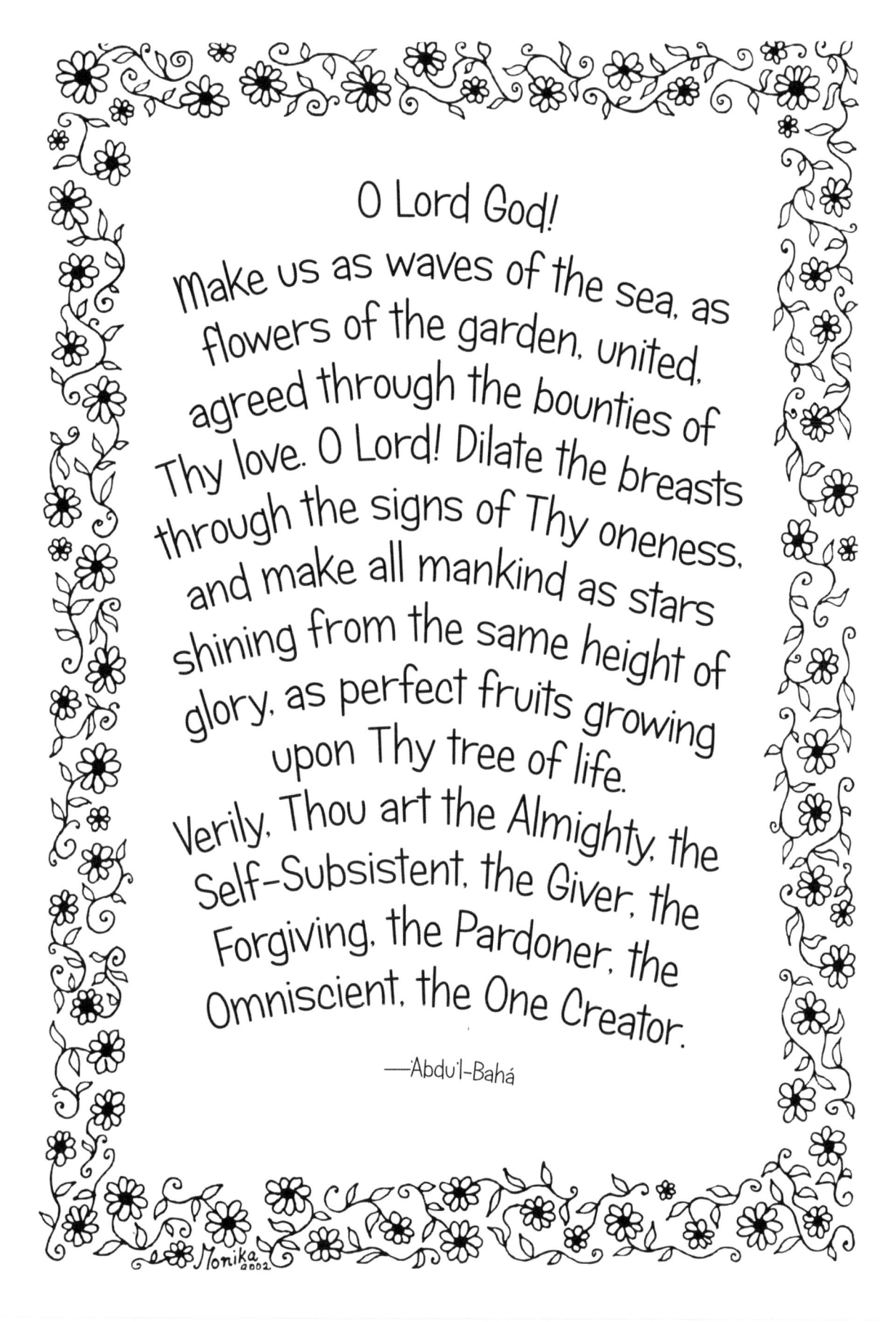

Make us as waves of the sea, as flowers of the garden, united, agreed through the bounties of Thy love. O Lord! Dilate the breasts through the signs of Thy oneness, and make all mankind as stars shining from the same height of glory, as perfect fruits growing upon Thy tree of life.

Verily, Thou art the Almighty, the Self-Subsistent, the Giver, the Forgiving, the Pardoner, the Omniscient, the One Creator.

—'Abdu'l-Bahá

The advent of the prophets and the revelation of the Holy Books is intended to create love between souls and friendship between the inhabitants of the earth.

'Abdu'l-Bahá

Thou seest Thy handmaiden, O My God, standing before the habitation of Thy Mercy, and calling upon Thee by Thy name which Thou hast chosen above all other names and set up over all that are in heaven and on earth. Send down upon her the breaths of Thy Mercy, that she may be carried away wholly from herself, and be drawn entirely towards the seat which, resplendent with the glory of Thy face, sheddeth afar the radiance of Thy sovereignty, and is established as Thy throne. Potent art Thou to do what Thou willest. No God is there beside Thee, the All-Glorious, the Most Bountiful.

Bahá'u'lláh

...strive ye to unite the hearts of those who follow other faiths....

'Abdu'l-Bahá

I am a child of tender years. Nourish me from the breast of Thy mercy, train me in the bosom of Thy love, educate me in the school of Thy guidance and develop me under the shadow of Thy bounty. Deliver me from darkness, make me a brilliant light; free me from unhappiness, make me a flower of the rose garden; suffer me to become a servant of Thy threshold and confer upon me the disposition and nature of the righteous; make me a cause of bounty to the human world, and crown my head with the diadem of eternal life.

Verily, Thou art the Powerful, the Mighty, the Seer, the Hearer.

– 'Abdu'l-Bahá

His fundamental purpose in enduring that continual toil and pain, and bearing those calamities, was to safeguard the divine and all-embracing Word, to shelter the tree of unity, to educate persons of capacity, to refine those who were pure in heart, and to transform the hearts of the receptive, to expound the mysteries of God and illumine the minds of the spiritual.

Bahíyyih Khánum,

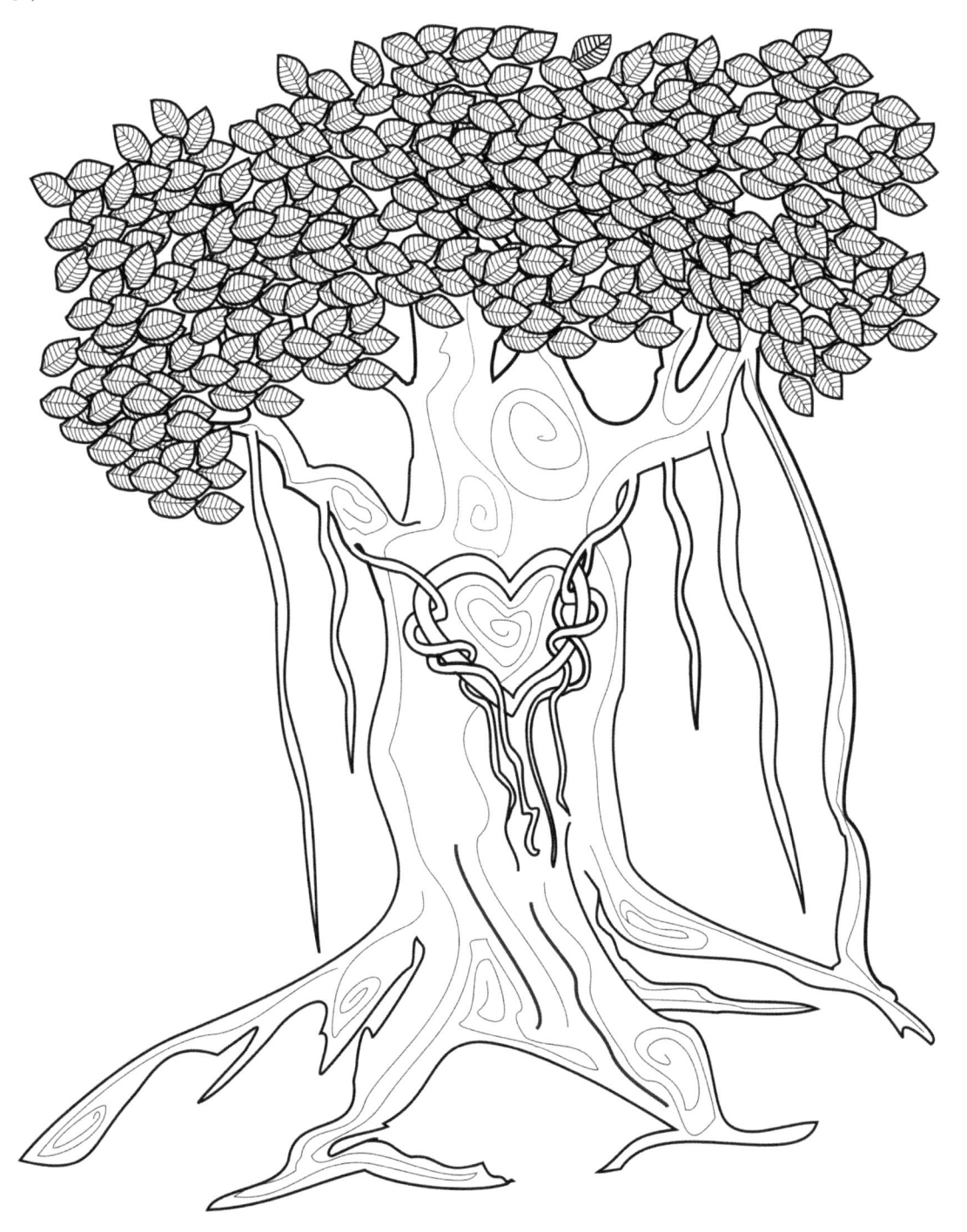

> Then, O ye friends of God! Ye must not only have kind and merciful feelings for mankind, but ye should also exercise the utmost kindness towards every living creature.
> 'Abdu'l-Bahá

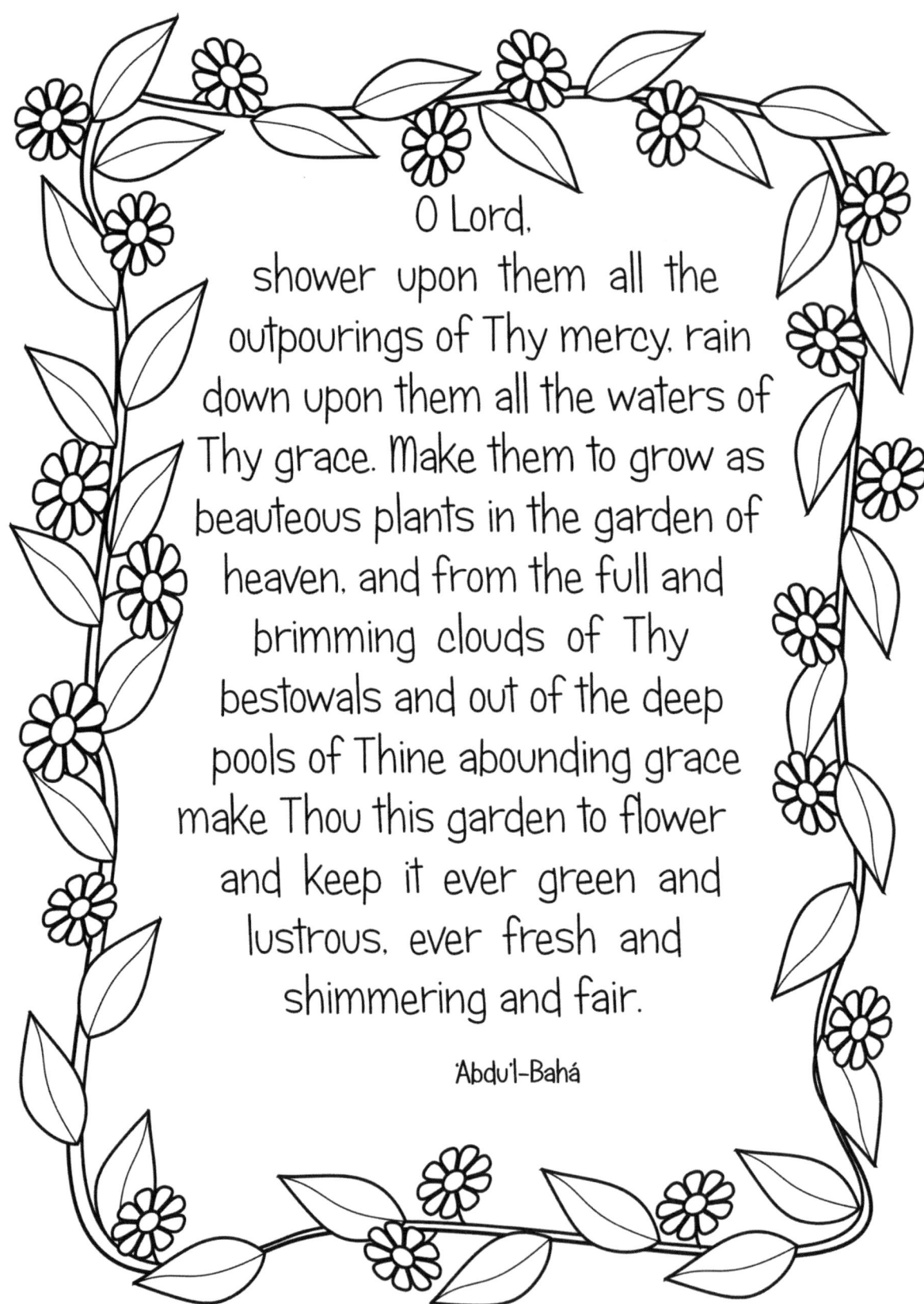

O Lord, shower upon them all the outpourings of Thy mercy, rain down upon them all the waters of Thy grace. Make them to grow as beauteous plants in the garden of heaven, and from the full and brimming clouds of Thy bestowals and out of the deep pools of Thine abounding grace make Thou this garden to flower and keep it ever green and lustrous, ever fresh and shimmering and fair.

'Abdu'l-Bahá

Why has God sent the prophets? It is self-evident that the prophets are the educators of men and the teachers of the human race.

'Abdu'l-Bahá

The human teeth, the molars, are formed to grind grain. The front teeth, the incisors, are for fruits, etc. It is, therefore, quite apparent according to the implements for eating that man's food is intended to be grain and not meat. When mankind is more fully developed, the eating of meat will gradually cease. — 'Abdu'l-Bahá

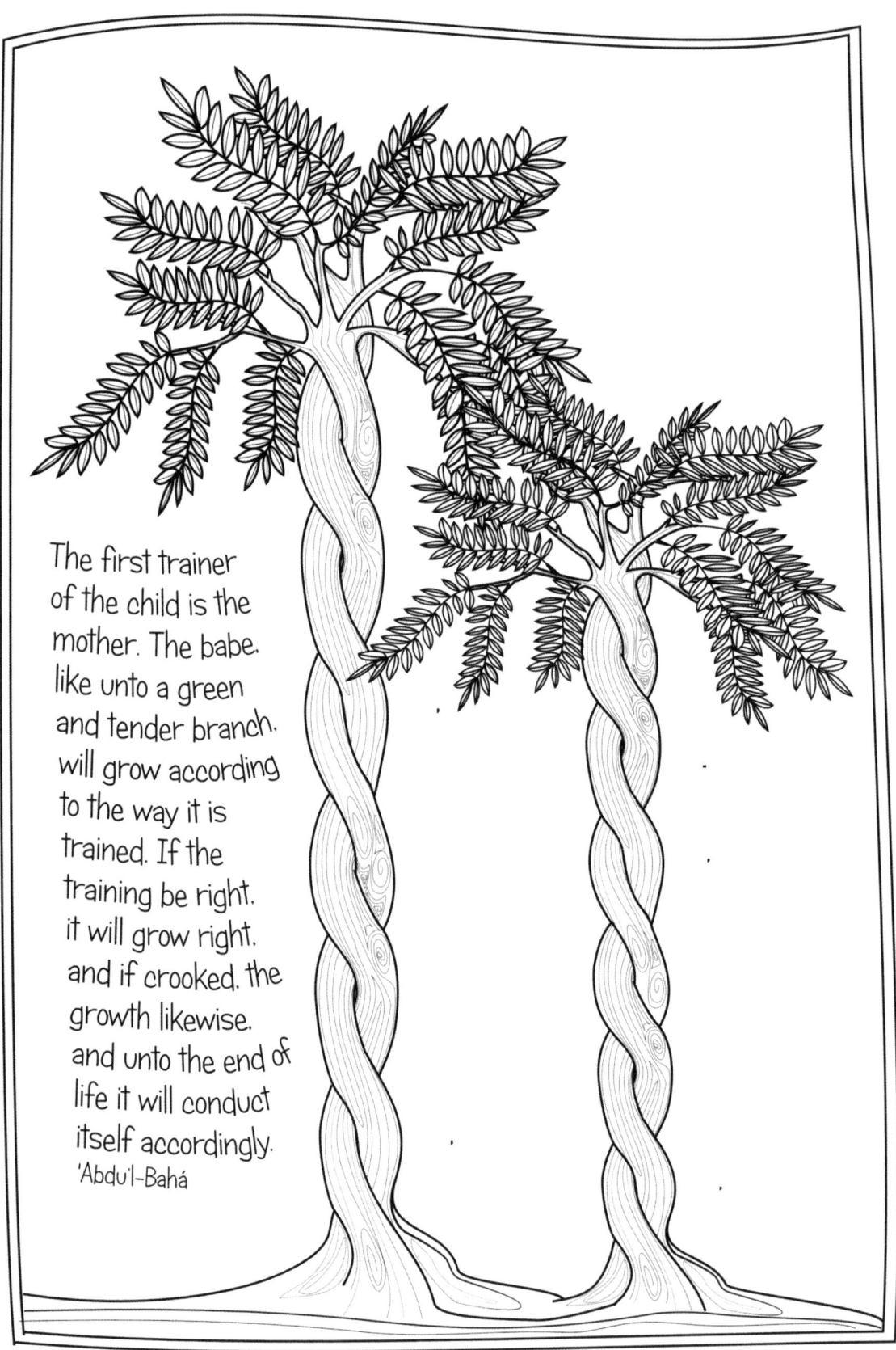

The first trainer of the child is the mother. The babe, like unto a green and tender branch, will grow according to the way it is trained. If the training be right, it will grow right, and if crooked, the growth likewise, and unto the end of life it will conduct itself accordingly.
'Abdu'l-Bahá

Verily, I pray God to make thy home a center for the radiation of light and the glowing of His love in the hearts of His people.
—'Abdu'l-Bahá

The instruction of these children is even as the work of a loving gardener who tendeth his young plants in the flowering fields of the All-Glorious.

'Abdu'l-Bahá

Ponder a while those holy words in your heart, and, with utter detachment, strive to grasp their meaning.

Bahá'u'lláh

The clouds of divine mercy are raining down their priceless jewels. The zephyrs of a new and divine springtime are wafting their fragrant breaths from the invisible world. Know ye then the value of these days.
'Abdu'l-Bahá

right thought
right thought
right speech
right speech
right action
right action

If love and agreement are manifest in a single family, that family will advance, become illumined and spiritual; but if enmity and hatred exist within it destruction and dispersion are inevitable. 'Abdu'l-Bahá

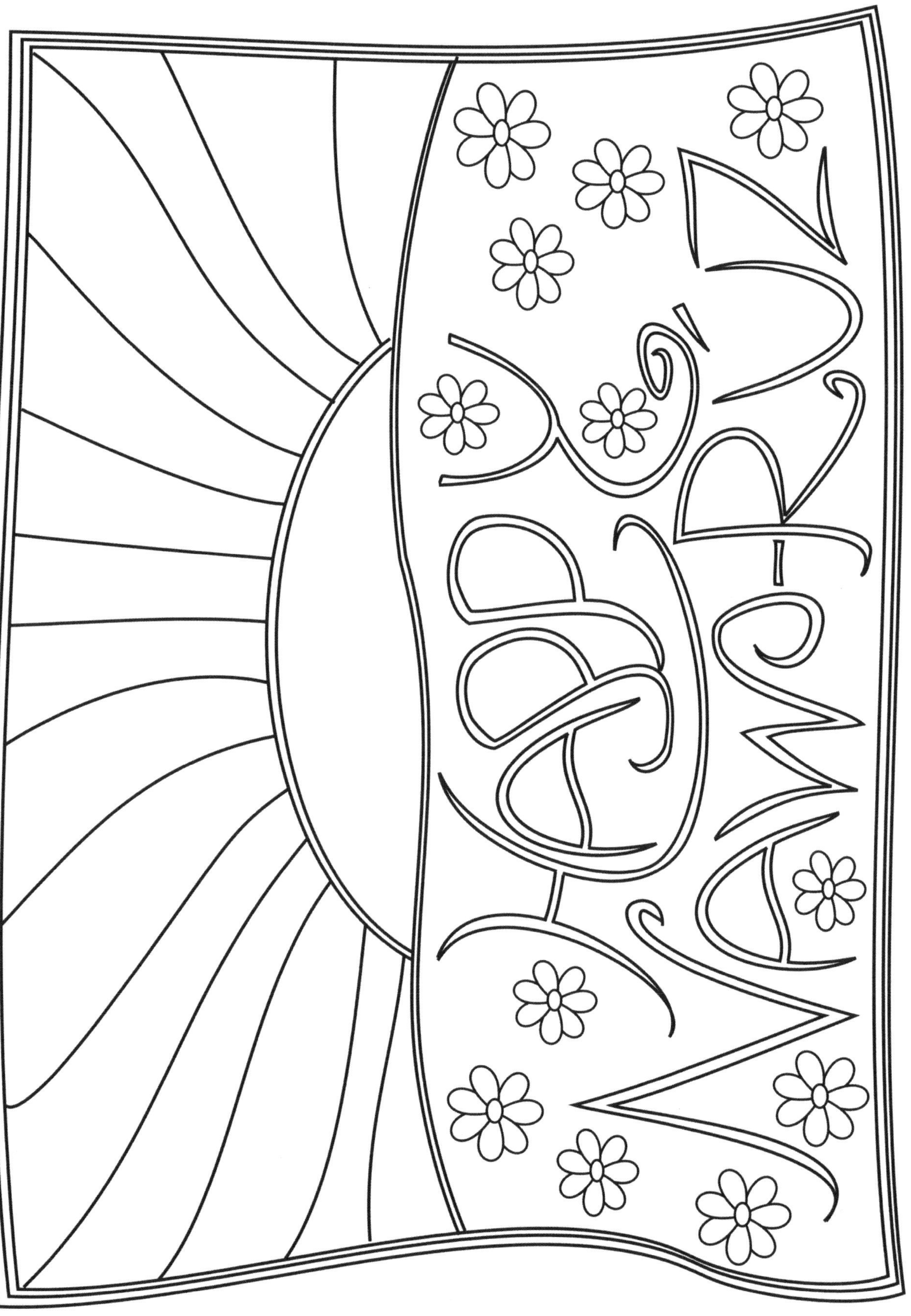
HAPPY
NAW-RÚZ

When love is realized and the ideal spiritual bonds unite the hearts of men, the whole human race will be uplifted, the world will continually grow more spiritual and radiant and the happiness and tranquillity of mankind be immeasurably increased.
'Abdu'l-Bahá

Man is a child of God, most noble, lofty and beloved by God his Creator. Therefore he must ever strive that the divine bounties and virtues bestowed upon him may prevail and control him. Just now the soil of human hearts seems like black earth, but in the innermost substance of this dark soil there are thousands of fragrant flowers latent. We must endeavour to cultivate and awaken these potentialities, discover the secret treasure in this very mine and depository of God, bring forth these resplendent powers long hidden in human hearts... 'Abdu'l-Bahá

44

All humankind are as children in a school, and the Dawning-Points of Light, the Sources of divine revelation, are the teachers.

'Abdu'l-Bahá

Let them purify their sight and behold all humankind as leaves and blossoms and fruits of the tree of being. Let them at all times concern themselves with doing a kindly thing for one of their fellows, offering to someone love, consideration, thoughtful help. 'Abdu'l-Bahá

"...... become the lighthouse of guidance......"
'Abdu'l-Bahá

With me thou art beloved and I ask God that thou mayest become the lighthouse of guidance in those regions and that thou mayest shine with the lights of oneness in this world of man.
- Abdu'l-Bahá

We ask God to endow human souls with justice so that they may be fair.
'Abdu'l-Bahá

He must do good to every soul whom he encounters....
'Abdu'l-Bahá

O friends, consort with all the people of the world with joy and fragrance.
'Abdu'l-Bahá

O Lord, shower upon them all the outpourings of Thy mercy, rain down upon them all the waters of Thy grace. Make them to grow as beauteous plants in the garden of heaven...

'Abdu'l-Bahá

We are drops of one ocean... We are leaves of one tree. Come and join us in our quest for unity

Hi, I'm a bad bitch

Spiritual progress is through the breaths of the Holy Spirit and is the awakening of the conscious soul of man to perceive the reality of Divinity.

'Abdu'l-Bahá

Be kind to all peoples;
care for every person;
do all ye can to purify the hearts and minds of men;
strive ye to gladden every soul.

—'Abdu'l-Bahá

It is incumbent upon all the peoples of the world to reconcile their differences, and, with perfect unity and peace, abide beneath the shadow of the Tree of His care and loving-kindness.

Bahá'u'lláh

Among the greatest of all great services is the education of children, and promotion of the various sciences, crafts and arts.

......through the restoring waters of pure intention and unselfish effort, the earth of human potentialities will blossom with its own latent excellence and flower into praiseworthy qualities, and bear and flourish ....

'Abdu'l-Bahá

The seed of reality must be sown again in human hearts in order that a new tree may grow therefrom and new divine fruits refresh the world.

'Abdu'l-Bahá

We must strive with energies of heart, soul and mind to develop and manifest the perfections and virtues latent within the realities of the phenomenal world, for the human reality may be compared to a seed. If we sow the seed, a mighty tree appears from it. The virtues of the seed are revealed in the tree: it puts forth branches, leaves, blossoms, and produces fruits. All these virtues were hidden and potential in the seed. Through the blessing and bounty of cultivation these virtues became apparent. Similarly the merciful God our creator has deposited within human realities certain virtues latent and potential. Through education and culture, these virtues deposited by the loving God will become apparent in the human reality even as the unfoldment of the tree from within the germinating seed. 'Abdu'l-Bahá

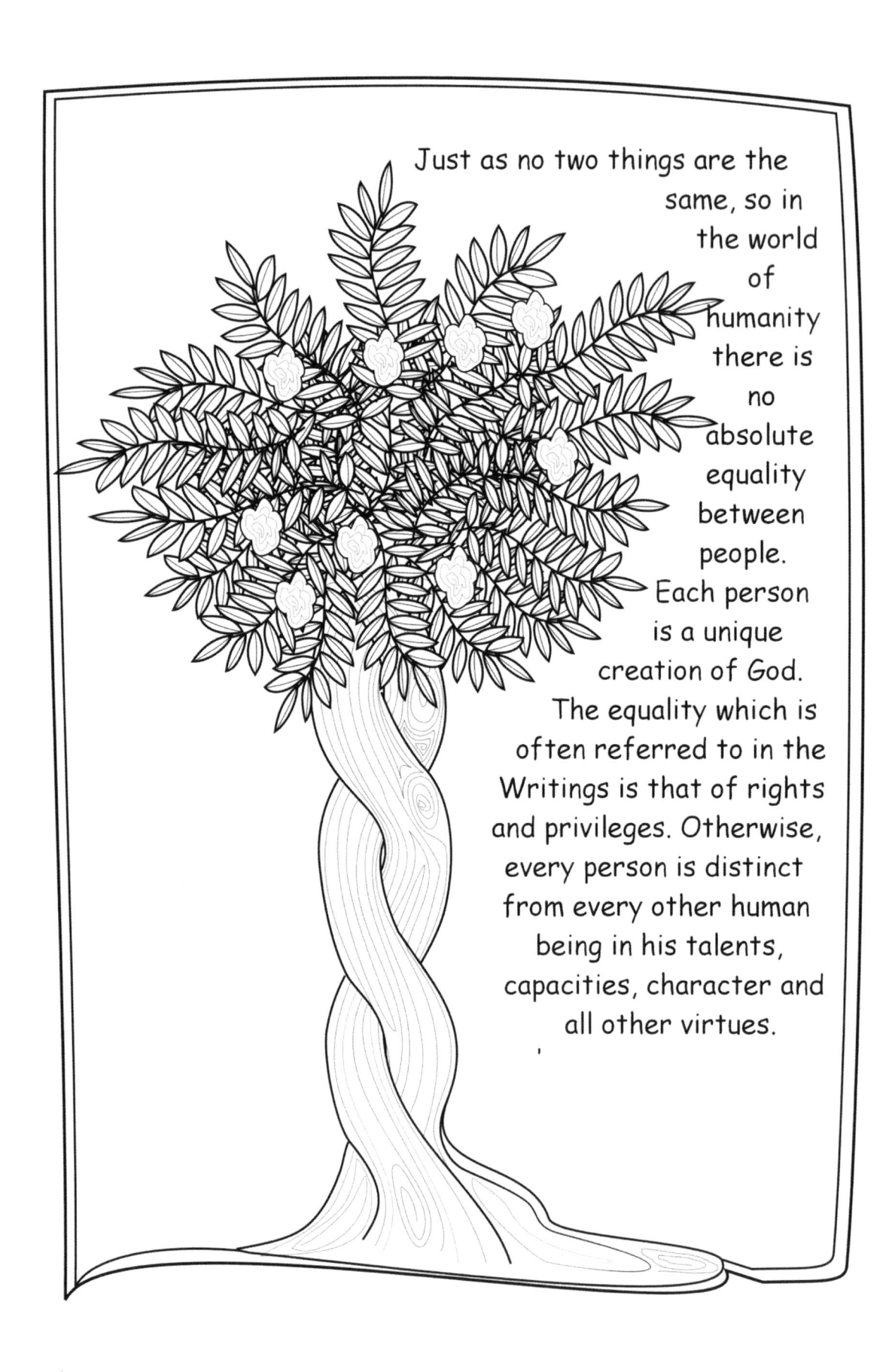

Just as no two things are the same, so in the world of humanity there is no absolute equality between people. Each person is a unique creation of God. The equality which is often referred to in the Writings is that of rights and privileges. Otherwise, every person is distinct from every other human being in his talents, capacities, character and all other virtues.

To every human being must ye be infinitely kind.
'Abdu'l-Bahá

...cheer ye every heart.
'Abdu'l-Bahá

...observe courtesy, for above all else it is the prince of virtues.
Bahá'u'lláh

...be even as a candle casting its light,....
'Abdu'l-Bahá

I am, O my God, Thy servant and the son of Thy servant. I have recognized Thy truth in Thy days, and have directed my steps towards the shores of Thy oneness, confessing Thy singleness, acknowledging Thy unity, and hoping for Thy forgiveness and pardon. Powerful art Thou to do what Thou willest; no God is there beside Thee, the All-Glorious, the Ever-Forgiving.

Bahá'u'lláh

........draw us nigh unto the shores of the ocean of Thy grace.
Bahá'u'lláh

To:
Thank you for teaching us. Teachers are very important and we appreciate you.

From

..."the children of men are in need of education and civilization, and they require to be polished, till they become bright and shining."
'Abdu'l-Bahá

Education makes the ignorant wise, the tyrant just, promotes happiness, strengthens the mind, develops the will and makes fruitless trees of humanity fruitful.
'Abdu'l-Bahá

Happy World Teachers' Day

To: Thank you for teaching us. Teachers are very important and we appreciate you.

From

"...the children of men are in need of education and civilization, and they require to be polished, till they become bright and shining."
Abdu'l-Bahá

Education makes the ignorant wise, the tyrant just, promotes happiness, strengthens the mind, develops the will and makes fruitless trees of humanity fruitful.
Abdu'l-Bahá

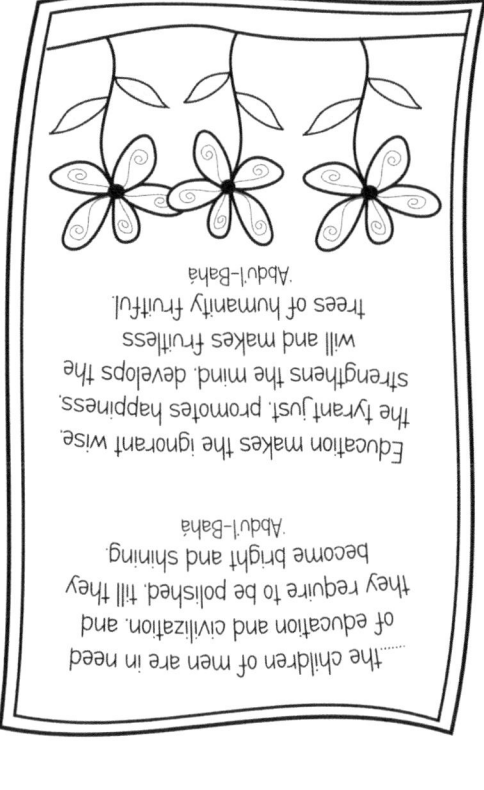

Happy World Teachers' Day

I hope thou shalt be a child of the Kingdom, shalt learn sciences, arts, and significances, may become a full grown tree, fruitful and green in the vineyard of God and be happy and full of cheer through the showers of the clouds of paradise.
'Abdu'l-Bahá

.......bestir yourselves, do all in your power to be as one, to live in peace, each with the others: for ye are all the drops from but one ocean, the foliage of one tree, the pearls from a single shell, the flowers and sweet herbs from the same one garden. And achieving that, strive ye to unite the hearts of those who follow other faiths. 'Abdu'l-Bahá

The Word of God may be likened unto a sapling, whose roots have been implanted in the hearts of men. It is incumbent upon you to foster its growth through the living waters of wisdom, of sanctified and holy words, so that its root may become firmly fixed and its branches may spread out as high as the heavens and beyond.

Bahá'u'lláh

Verily, I supplicate to God to make thee sincere in this love, to illumine thee with the light of His Kingdom,and to destine unto thee the illumination by the light of His attributes, to make thee a sign of mercy, a bird warbling the verses of unity; that thou mayest be nurtured in the bosom of His providence, and become a growing tree bearing fruit in the Paradise of El-Abha. -Abdu'l-Bahá

"O friends, consort with all the people of the world with joy and fragrance."
‘Abdu'l-Bahá

O Lord!
Unite and bind
together the
hearts, join in
accord
all the souls,
and exhilarate
the spirits through
the signs of Thy
sanctity
and oneness.

'Abdu'l-Bahá

O my God! O my God! Unite the hearts of Thy servants, and reveal to them Thy great purpose. May they follow Thy commandments and abide in Thy law. Help them, O God, in their endeavour, and grant them strength to serve Thee. O God! Leave them not to themselves, but guide their steps by the light of Thy knowledge, and cheer their hearts by Thy love. Verily, Thou art their Helper and their Lord. – Bahá'u'lláh

May the trees of your hearts bring forth new leaves and variegated blossoms. May ideal fruits appear from them in order that the world of humanity, which has grown and developed in material civilization, may be quickened in the bringing forth of spiritual ideals.

'Abdu'l-Bahá

O SON OF BEING!

With the hands of power I made thee and with the fingers of strength I created thee; and within thee have I placed the essence of My light.

Bahá'u'lláh

Ye must become brilliant lamps. Ye must shine as stars radiating the light of love toward all mankind. May you be the cause of love amongst the nations.

'Abdu'l-Bahá

God is one; the effulgence of God is one; and humanity constitutes the servants of that one God. God is kind to all. He creates and provides for all; and all are under His care and protection.

The Sun of Truth, the Word of God shines upon all mankind; the divine cloud pours down its precious rain; the gentle zephyrs of His mercy blow and all humanity is submerged in the ocean of His eternal justice and loving-kindness.

'Abdu'l-Bahá

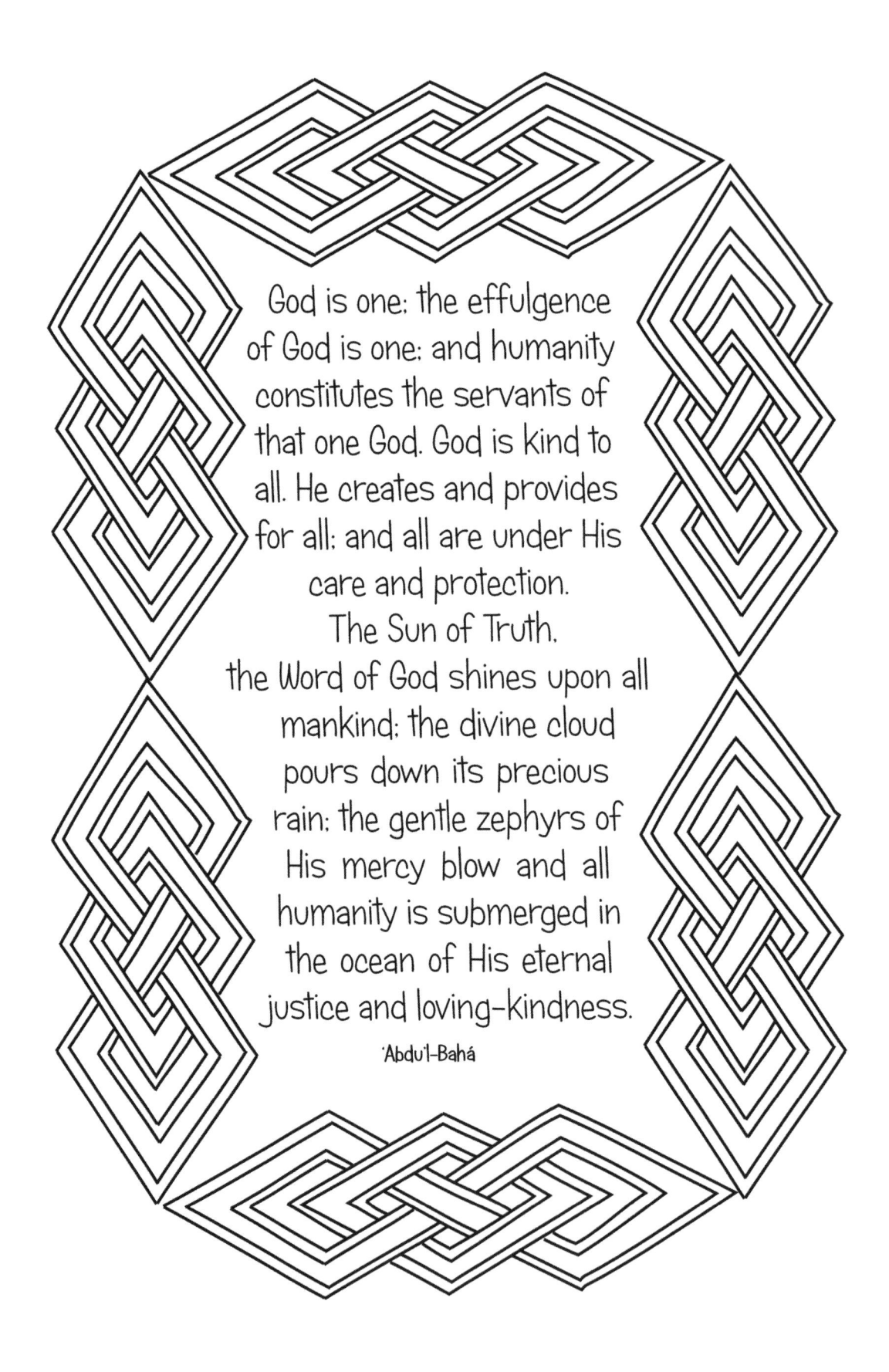

Be unto the world as rain and clouds of mercy, as suns of truth, be a celestial army, and you shall indeed conquer the city of hearts.

'Abdu'l-Bahá

True civilization will unfurl its banner in the midmost heart of the world whenever a certain number of its distinguished and high-minded sovereigns -- the shining exemplars of devotion and determination -- shall, for the good and happiness of all mankind, arise, with firm resolve and clear vision, to establish the Cause of Universal Peace.
'Abdu'l-Bahá

Open the doors of your hearts.
Bahá'u'lláh

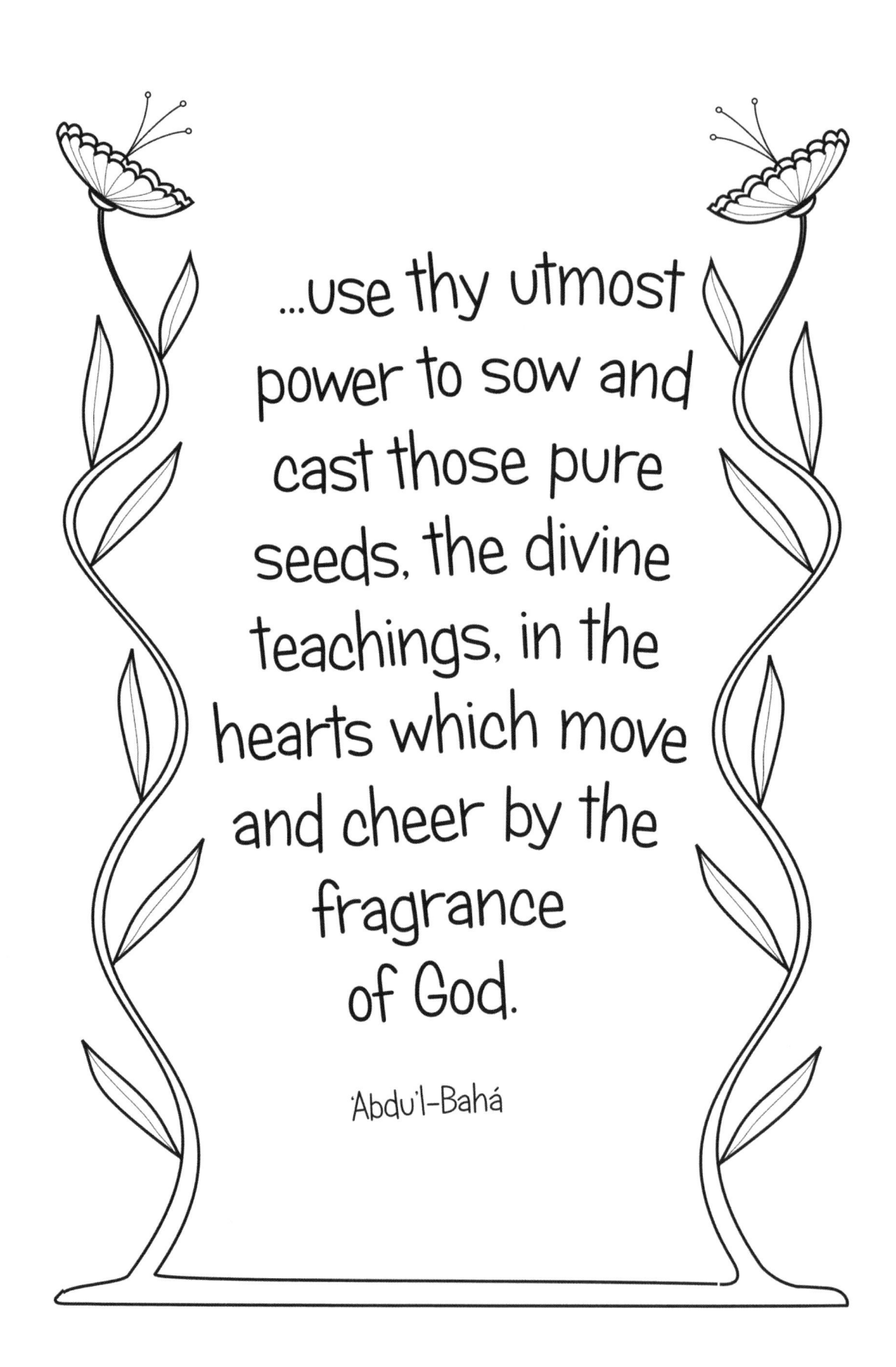

...use thy utmost power to sow and cast those pure seeds, the divine teachings, in the hearts which move and cheer by the fragrance of God.

'Abdu'l-Bahá

> We ask God to endow human souls with justice so that they may be fair, and may strive to provide for the comfort of all....

'Abdu'l-Bahá

Welcome to Peaceville

The purpose of God in creating man hath been, and will ever be, to enable him to know his Creator and to attain His Presence.
Bahá'u'lláh

In flower-spangled meadows hath the divine springtime pitched its tents, and the spiritual are inhaling sweet scents from the Sheba of the spirit, carried their way by the east wind.

'Abdu'l-Bahá

O friends! Be not careless of the virtues with which ye have been endowed, neither be neglectful of your high destiny.

Bahá'u'lláh

You must deal with all in loving-kindness in order that this precious seed entrusted to your planting may continue to grow and bring forth its perfect fruit.
'Abdu'l-Bahá

O Lord! Make this youth radiant, and confer Thy bounty upon this poor creature. Bestow upon him knowledge, grant him added strength at the break of every morn and guard him within the shelter of Thy protection so that he may be freed from error, may devote himself to the service of Thy Cause, may guide the wayward, lead the hapless, free the captives and awaken the heedless, that all may be blessed with Thy remembrance and praise.
Thou art the Mighty and the Powerful.   - 'Abdu'l-Bahá

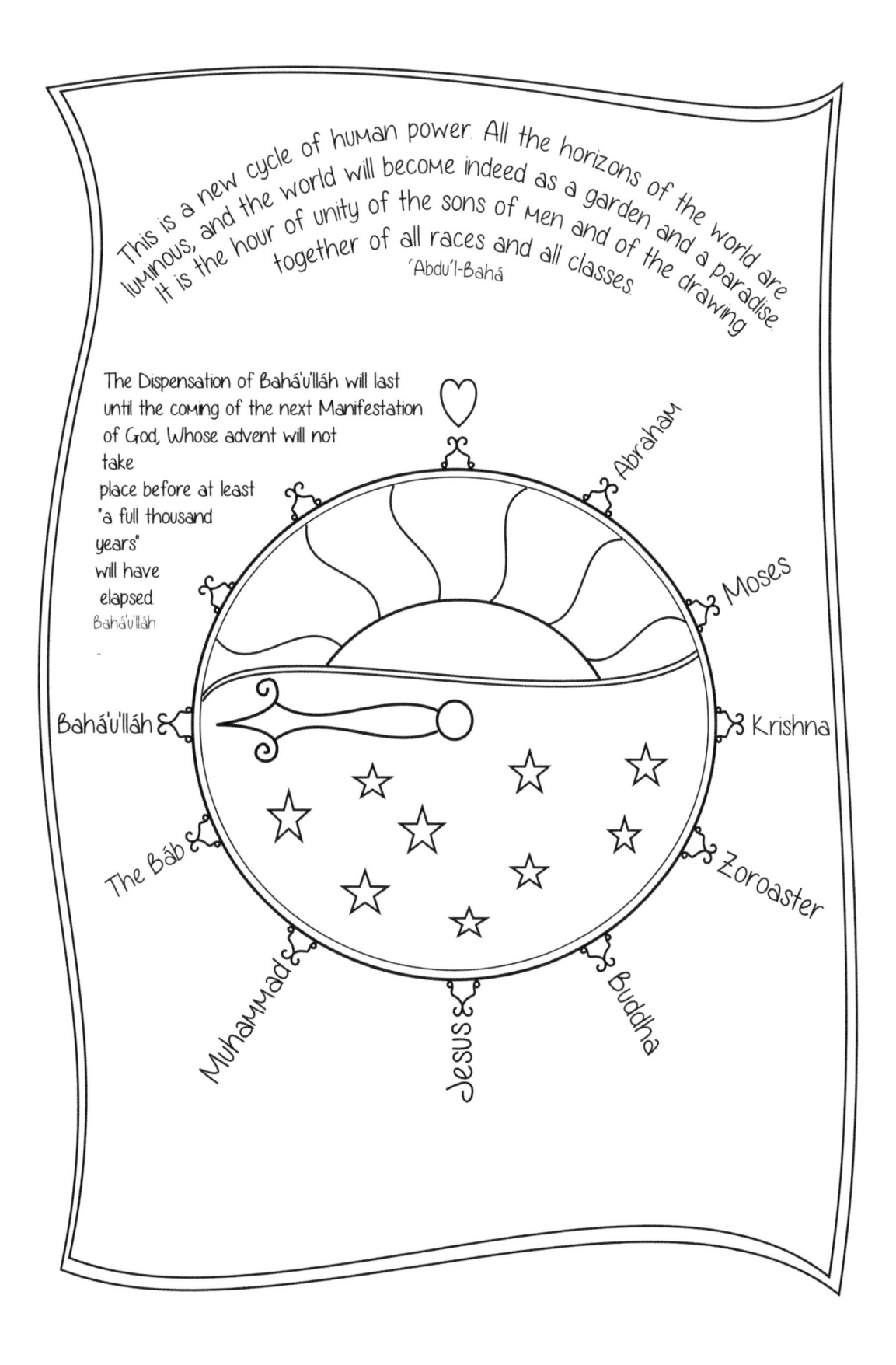

> This is a new cycle of human power. All the horizons of the world are luminous, and the world will become indeed as a garden and a paradise. It is the hour of unity of the sons of men and of the drawing together of all races and all classes.
> — 'Abdu'l-Bahá

The Dispensation of Bahá'u'lláh will last until the coming of the next Manifestation of God, Whose advent will not take place before at least "a full thousand years" will have elapsed
— Bahá'u'lláh

- Abraham
- Moses
- Krishna
- Zoroaster
- Buddha
- Jesus
- Muhammad
- The Báb
- Bahá'u'lláh

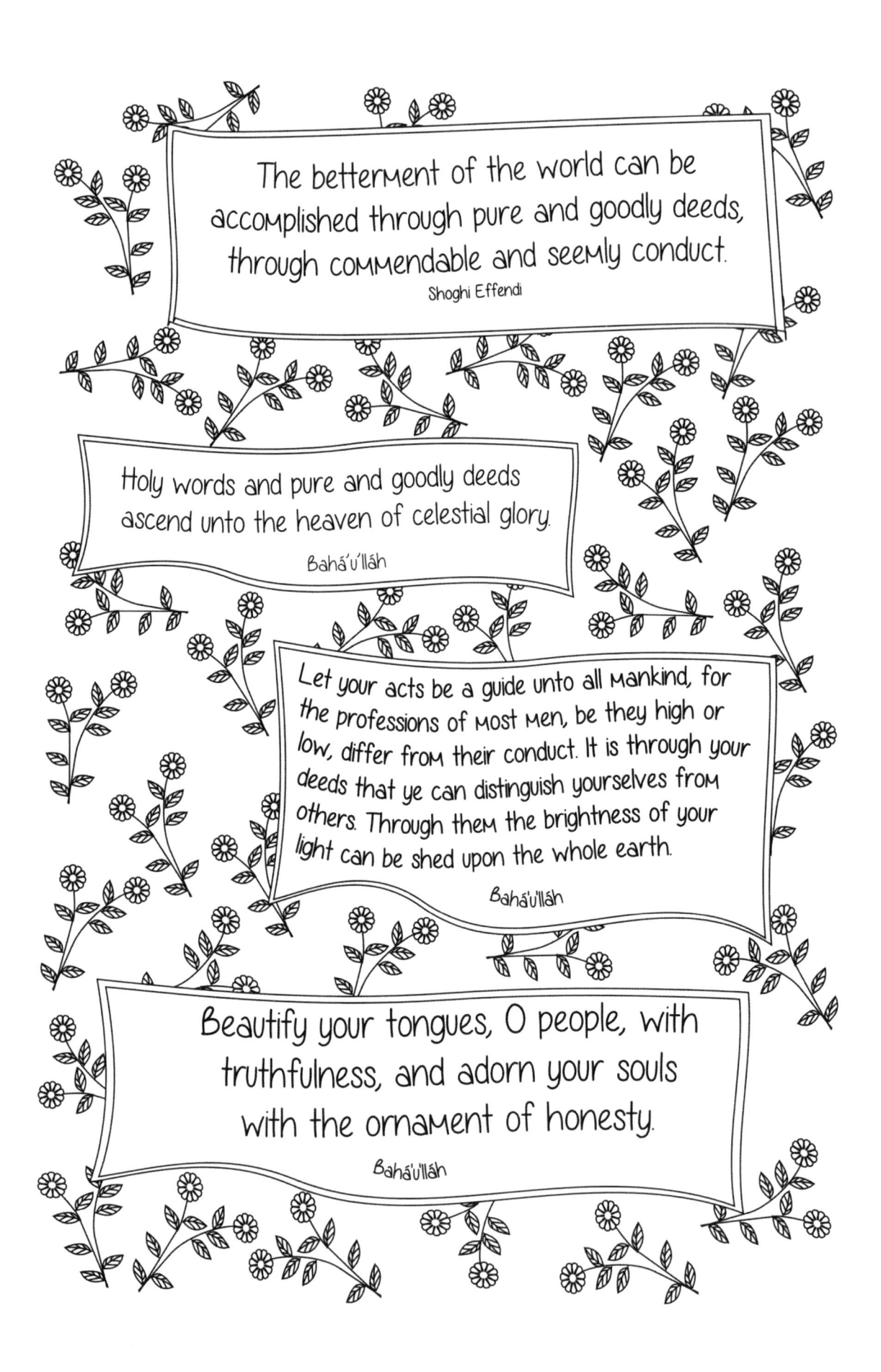

The betterment of the world can be accomplished through pure and goodly deeds, through commendable and seemly conduct.
Shoghi Effendi

Holy words and pure and goodly deeds ascend unto the heaven of celestial glory.
Bahá'u'lláh

Let your acts be a guide unto all mankind, for the professions of most men, be they high or low, differ from their conduct. It is through your deeds that ye can distinguish yourselves from others. Through them the brightness of your light can be shed upon the whole earth.
Bahá'u'lláh

Beautify your tongues, O people, with truthfulness, and adorn your souls with the ornament of honesty.
Bahá'u'lláh

O SON OF MAN! Rejoice in the gladness of thine heart, that thou mayest be worthy to meet Me and to mirror forth My beauty

Bahá'u'lláh

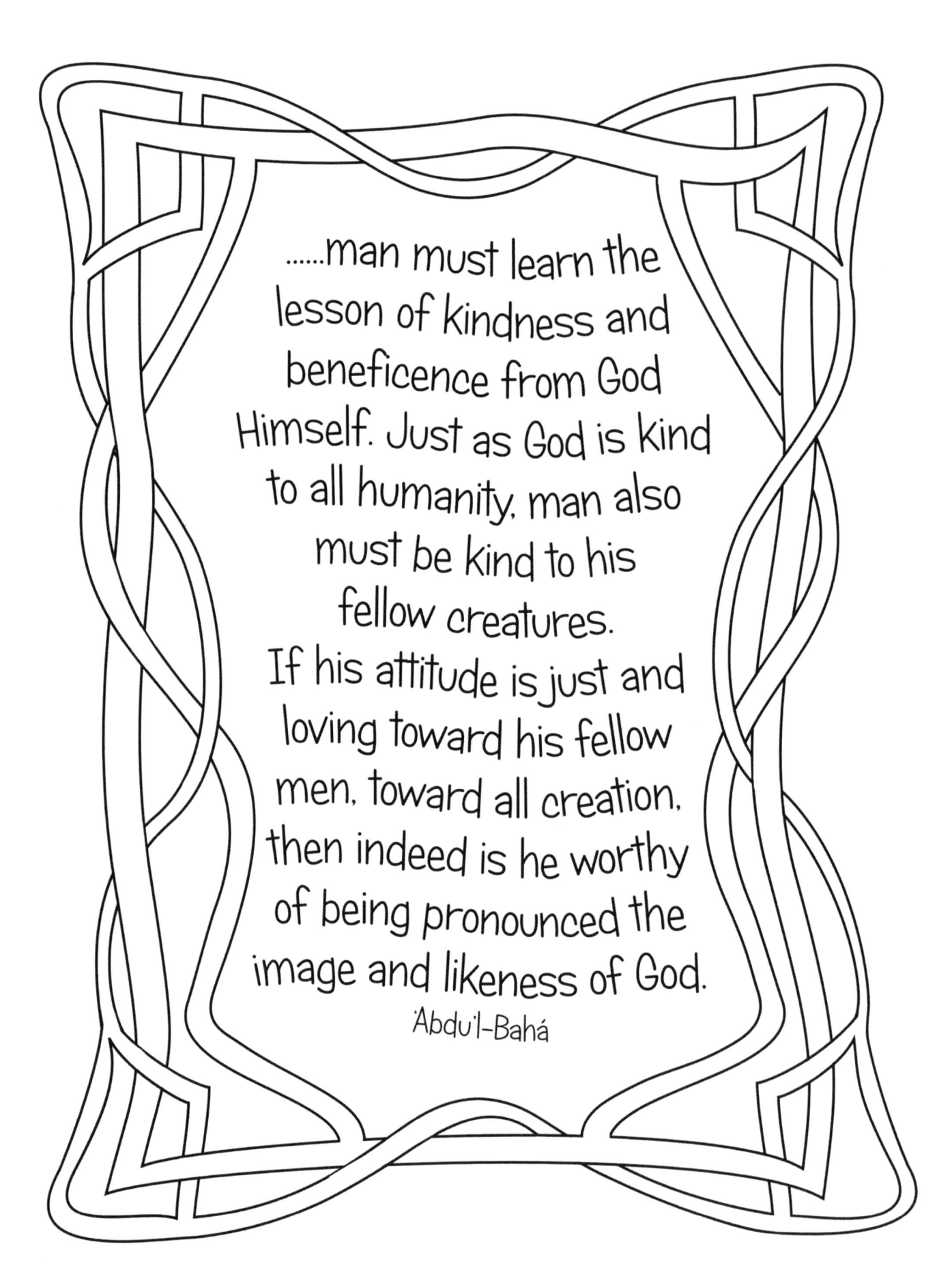

......man must learn the lesson of kindness and beneficence from God Himself. Just as God is kind to all humanity, man also must be kind to his fellow creatures.
If his attitude is just and loving toward his fellow men, toward all creation, then indeed is he worthy of being pronounced the image and likeness of God.
'Abdu'l-Bahá

Shine out like the day-star, be unresting as the sea; even as the clouds of heaven, shed ye life upon field and hill, and like unto April winds, blow freshness through those human trees, and bring them to their blossoming.
'Abdu'l-Bahá

Ye must therefore put forth a mighty effort, striving by night and day and resting not for a moment, to acquire an abundant share of all the sciences and arts, that the Divine Image, which shineth out from the Sun of Truth, may illumine the mirror of the hearts of men.
'Abdu'l-Bahá

Work for the day of Universal Peace.
Strive always that you may be united.
Kindness and love in the path of service
must be your means.
'Abdu'l-Bahá

Community Garden

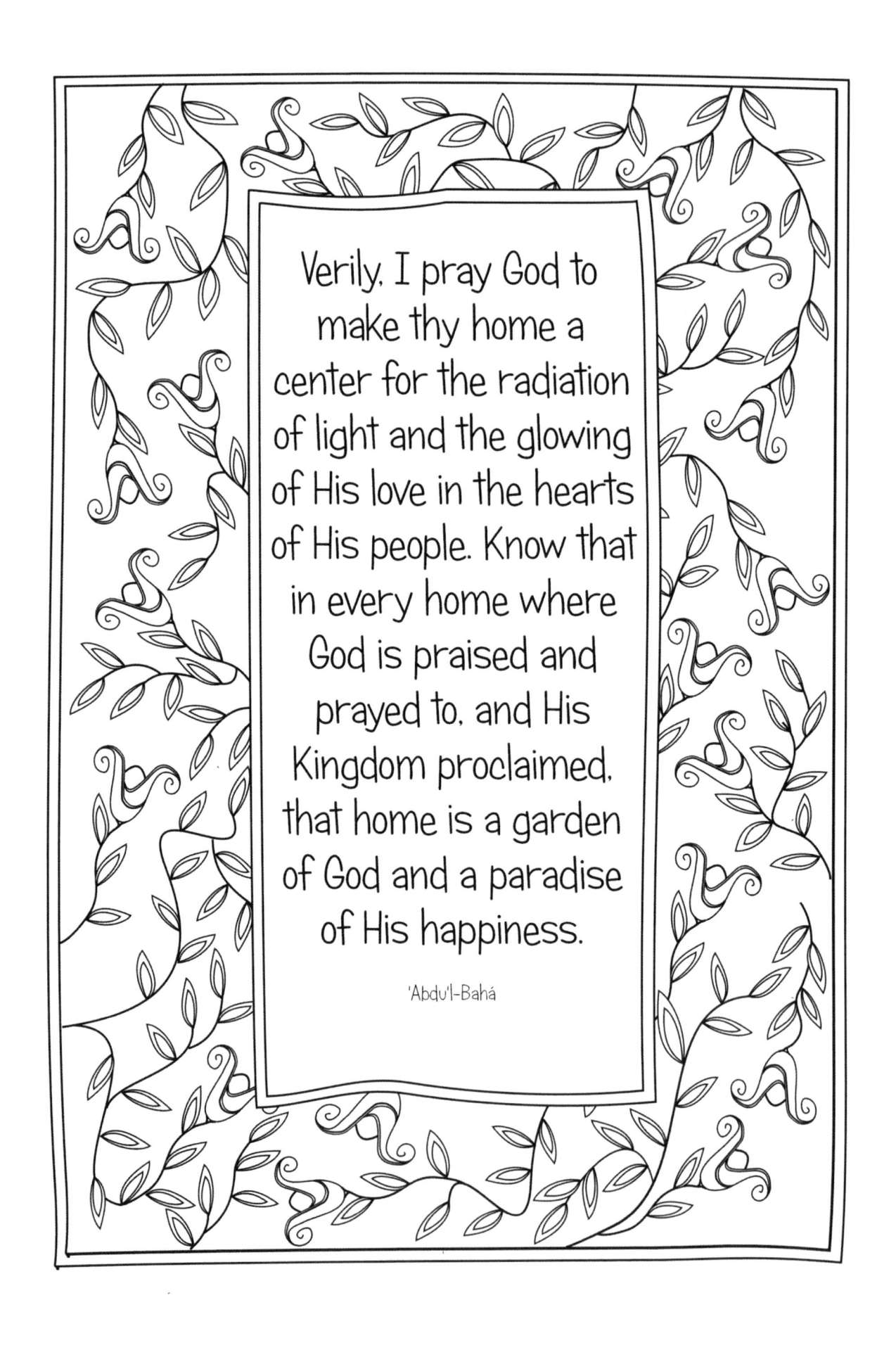

Verily, I pray God to make thy home a center for the radiation of light and the glowing of His love in the hearts of His people. Know that in every home where God is praised and prayed to, and His Kingdom proclaimed, that home is a garden of God and a paradise of His happiness.

'Abdu'l-Bahá

From the horizon of detachment Thou hast manifested souls that, even as the shining moon, shed radiance upon the realm of heart and soul.
'Abdu'l-Bahá

The most important thing is to polish the mirrors of hearts in order that they may become illumined and receptive of the divine light.
'Abdu'l-Bahá

The instruction of these children is even as the work of a loving gardener who tendeth his young plants in the flowering fields of the All-Glorious.
'Abdu'l-Bahá

The babe, like unto a green and tender branch, will grow according to the way it is trained.

'Abdu'l-Bahá

Say: God sufficeth all things above all things, and nothing in the heavens or in the earth but God sufficeth. Verily, He is in Himself the Knower, the Sustainer, the Omnipotent.

The Báb

Strive, therefore, with heart and soul that ye become ignited candles in the assemblage of the world

'Abdu'l-Bahá

We must now highly resolve to arise and lay hold of all those instrumentalities that promote the peace and well-being and happiness, the knowledge, culture and industry, the dignity, value and station, of the entire human race. Thus, through the restoring waters of pure intention and unselfish effort, the earth of human potentialities will blossom with its own latent excellence and flower.

'Abdu'l-Bahá

References for quotes from Bahá'í Reference Library

P 2 *"O God, make our souls.."* 'Abdu'l-Bahá, Selections from the Writings of 'Abdu'l-Bahá, 42.

p. 3 *"Turn all your thoughts…."* 'Abdu'l-Bahá, The Promulgation of Universal Peace, 134.
Home of Mr. and Mrs. Edward B. Kinney

p. 4 *"All the virtues which have been deposited…"* 'Abdu'l-Bahá, The Promulgation of Universal Peace, 15 Studio Hall

P. 5 *"Gather all people…"* 'Abdu'l-Bahá, The Promulgation of Universal Peace, 46. Unity Church.

p. 6 *"O Thou Peerless Lord! Let this suckling babe… "* Bahá'í Prayers: A Selection of Prayers Revealed by Bahá'u'lláh, the Báb and 'Abdu'l-Bahá p. 33

p. 7 Bookmarks *" O People of the world."* 'Abdu'l-Bahá A Traveller's Narrative.
"What then is the mission of the divine Prophets?.."
'Abdu'l-Bahá, The Promulgation of Universal Peace, 112. Temple Emmanu-El
"The fruits of the human tree" Bahá'u'lláh / *"This Wronged One doth mention him who hath set his…"*

p.9 Bookmarks *"I bear witness, O my God,.."* Bahá'u'lláh / The Kitáb-i-Aqdas, Short Obligatory Prayer
"Ye are the saplings.." Bahá'u'lláh / Epistle to the Son of the Wolf
"Whoso reciteth..." Bahá'u'lláh, Gleanings from the Writings of Bahá'u'lláhCXXXVI:
"Say: Deliver your souls, O people, from…"
"I pray God to give thee..." Tablets of Abdul-Baha Abbas, Pages 87-89: gr6

p.10 Bookmarks *"Man is like unto a tree.."* Bahá'u'lláh, Tablets of Bahá'u'lláh
"This Wronged One doth mention him who hath set his…"
"Bestir yourselves," 'Abdu'l-Bahá, Selections from the Writings of 'Abdu'l-Bahá, 221:
"O ye who are steadfast in the Covenant! The…"
"The gentle breeze…." 'Abdu'l-Bahá, Selections from the Writings of 'Abdu'l-Bahá, 204
"O phoenix of that immortal flame kindled in the…"
"Verily I pray God..." 'Abdu'l-Bahá, Tablets of Abdul-Baha Abbas, Pages 68-69: gr5

p.13 *"Say: No man can attain.."* Baha'u'llah quoted in The Prosperity of Humankind, Pages 7-8: gr6

p.14 *"Whoso reciteth..."* Bahá'u'lláh, Gleanings from the Writings of Bahá'u'lláh,**CXXXVI:**
"Say: Deliver your souls, O people, from…"

P. 16 *"O Lord! Grant Thine.."* 'Abdu'l-Bahá Promulgation of Universal Peace 46. Unity Church

p. 17 *"O Lord God! Make our souls.."* and 'Abdu'l-Bahá Bahá'í Prayers: A Selection of Prayers Revealed by Bahá'u'lláh, the Báb, and 'Abdu'l-Bahá p. 206 207

p.18 *"The advent of the prophets…"* 'Abdu'l-Bahá, Tablets of Abdul-Baha Abbas, Page 505: gr2

p. 19 *"The great being saith.."* Bahá'u'lláh, Gleanings from the Writings of Bahá'u'lláh, CXXII:
"Man is the supreme Talisman. Lack of a…"

p. 20 *"O Lord, **brighten Thou** my face..."*, 'Abdu'l-Bahá, **Selections from the Writings of 'Abdu'l-Bahá** 146:
"O thou handmaid afire with the love of God! I…"

p. 21 *"Thou seest Thy handmaiden.."* Bahá'u'lláh, **Prayers and Meditations by Bahá'u'lláh** LXXXVII: "Magnified be Thy name, O Lord my God! Behold Thou mine eye expectant…"

p. 22 *"Strive ye to unite.."* 'Abdu'l-Bahá, Selections from the Writings of 'Abdu'l-Bahá, 221:
"O ye who are steadfast in the Covenant! The…"

p. 23 *"The Sun of Reality has dawned,.."* 'Abdu'l-Bahá, **The Promulgation of Universal Peace,** 43.
                                                            Sanatorium of Dr. C. M. Swingle

p. 24 *" I am a child of tender years."* 'Abdu'l-Bahá Bahá'í Prayers: A Selection of Prayers Revealed by
                                                          Bahá'u'lláh, the Báb, and 'Abdu'l-Bahá

p. 25 *"His fundamental purpose.."* Bahíyyih Khánum, the Greatest Holy Leaf:
                A Compilation from Bahá'í Sacred Texts
              and Writings of the Guardian of the Faith and Bahíyyih Khánum's
              Own Letters, 54: " The letter that you wrote in your burning …"

p. 26 *"Then, O ye friends of God!"* 'Abdu'l-Bahá, Bahá'í World Faith—Selected Writings of Bahá'u'lláh and
                                          'Abdu'l-Bahá ('Abdu'l-Bahá's Section Only)

p. 28 *"O Lord, shower upon them.."* 'Abdu'l-Bahá , Selections from the Writings of 'Abdu'l-Bahá, 8:
                              "O ye   beloved of 'Abdu'l-Bahá and ye handmaids of…"

p. 29 *"Why has God sent the prophets?"* 'Abdu'l-Bahá , The Promulgation of Universal Peace, 121.
                Eighth Street Temple, Synagogue or Foundations of World Unity, Pages 92-99: gr7

p.30 *"The human teeth…"* 'Abdu'l-Bahá The Promulgation of Universal Peace, 60. Church of the Ascension

p.31 *"Make me a cause of bounty.."* 'Abdu'l-Bahá, Baha'i Prayers: A Selection of Prayers Revealed by
                Baha'u'llah, the Bab, and `Abdu'l-Baha, Pages 37-38: 38

p.*32* *"The first trainer of the child is…"* 'Abdu'l-Bahá Tablets of Abdul-Baha Abbas

p.33 *"Verily, I pray God…"* 'Abdu'l-Bahá , Tablets of Abdul-Baha Abbas, Pages 68-69: gr5

p.34 *"Educate the children.."* : 'Abdu'l-Bahá , Selections from the Writings of 'Abdu'l-Bahá, 114:
                              "O ye loving mothers, know ye that in God's sight,…"

p. 35 *"The instruction of these children…"* 'Abdu'l-Bahá , Selections from the Writings of 'Abdu'l-Bahá, 123:
                                    "O thou who gazest upon the Kingdom of God!..."

p. 36 *" O ye children of men…"* Bahá'u'lláh , Tablets of Bahá'u'lláh/ 11. Lawḥ-i-Maqṣúd (Tablet of Maqṣúd)

p. 37 *"ponder a while…"* Bahá'u'lláh ,The Kitáb-i-Íqán / Part One

p. 38 *"The clouds of Divine mercy..."* 'Abdu'l-Bahá The Promulgation of Universal Peace 3.
                              Studio of Miss Phillips

p. 40 *"If love and agreement are manifest.."* 'Abdu'l-Bahá The Promulgation of Universal Peace, 54.
                                    Huntington Chambers

p. 42. *"When love is realized…"* 'Abdu'l-Bahá, The Promulgation of Universal Peace, 54.
                                    Huntington Chambers

p. 43 *"Man is a child of God."* 'Abdu'l-Bahá **,** The Promulgation of Universal Peace, 97.
                                    Home of Madame Morey

p. 45**.** *"All humankind are as…"*, 'Abdu'l-Bahá, Selections from Writings of Abdu'l-Bahá , 102.

p. 46 *"Let them purify their sight…"*, 'Abdu'l-Bahá, Selections from the Writings of Abdu'l-Baha', 1:
                                    "O peoples of the world! The Sun of Truth hath…"

p. 47 & 48 *"Lighthouse of guidance.."* 'Abdu'l-Bahá , Tablets of Abdul-Baha Abbas, Pages 343-344: 344

p. 49 *"He must do good..."* 'Abdu'l-Bahá , Baha'i World Faith – Selected Writings of Bahá'u'lláh, and 'Abdu'l-Bahá
                ('Abdu'l-Bahá's section only) Pages 215-217

    "O Friends, consort with.." 'Abdu'l-Bahá, A Traveller's Narrative
    "We ask God to endow…" 'Abdu'l-Bahá, 102. Coronation Hall, The Promulgation of Universal Peace

p.50 *"O Lord, shower upon them.."* 'Abdu'l-Bahá, 8: "O ye beloved of 'Abdu'l-Bahá and
                                        ye handmaids of…", Selections from the Writings of 'Abdu'l-Bahá

p. 53. *"Spiritual progress"* 'Abdu'l-Bahá , The Promulgation of Universal Peace, 52. Unitarian Conference

p*.* 54 *"Be kind to all peoples.."* 'Abdu'l-Bahá, Selections from the Writings of Abdu'l-Bahá, 200:
                              "O my spiritual loved ones! At a time when"

p. 55 *"It is incumbent…."* Bahá'u'lláh, Gleanings from the Writings of Bahá'u'lláh,
                / IV: "This is the Day in which God's most excellent…"

p. 56 *"Amongst the greatest.."* A Compilation on Baha'I Education, Page 27: gr4
p. 57 *" Through the restoring waters…."* 'Abdu'l-Bahá, The Secret of Divine Civilization

p. 58 *"The seed of reality…"* 'Abdu'l-Bahá, The Promulgation of Universal Peace, 52. Unitarian Conference
p. 59 *"We must strive with energies…"* 'Abdu'l-Bahá, The Promulgation of Universal Peace, 38.
    Theosophical Society
p. 60 *" Just as no two things are the same…"* Adib Taherzadeh, The Revelation of Bahá'u'lláh v 4, p. 199

p. 61 *"To every human being…"* 'Abdu'l-Bahá, Selections from the Writings of 'Abdu'l-Bahá, 221:
    "O ye who are steadfast in the Covenant! The…"
  "…cheer ye every heart.." 'Abdu'l-Bahá , Selections from the Writings of 'Abdu'l-Bahá, 16:
    "O ye illumined loved ones and ye handmaids of the…"
  "…observe courtesy.. " Bahá'u'lláh, Tablets of Bahá'u'lláh, 7. Lawḥ-i-Dunyá (Tablet of the World)
  "…be even as a candle…" 'Abdu'l-Bahá, Selections from the Writings of 'Abdu'l-Bahá, 17:

p. 62 *" I am, O My God…"* Bahá'u'lláh , Prayers and Meditations by Bahá'u'lláh, CXXXIV:
    "I am he, O my Lord, that hath set his face towards Thee, and fixed his…"
p. 63 *"Draw us nigh…"* Bahá'u'lláh , Gleanings from the Writings of Bahá'u'lláh, CXXXVIII:
    "Thou seest, O God of Mercy, Thou…
p. 64 . *"…the children of men are in need…"* 'Abdu'l-Bahá, 'Abdu'l-Baha in London, Pages 27-30: gr8
  "Education makes the ignorant…" 'Abdu'l-Bahá, The Promulgation of Universal Peace, 37. Hotel Plaza
p. 65 *"…the children of men are in need…"* 'Abdu'l-Bahá, 'Abdu'l-Baha in London, Pages 27-30: gr8
  "Education makes the ignorant…" 'Abdu'l-Bahá, The Promulgation of Universal Peace, 37. Hotel Plaza
p. 66 *" I hope thou shalt be…"* 'Abdu'l-Bahá,Tablets of Abdul-Baha Abbas, Page 68: gr3
p. 67 *"Bestir yourselves, …"* 'Abdu'l-Bahá, , Selections from the Writings of 'Abdu'l-Bahá, 221:
    "O ye who are steadfast in the Covenant! The…"
p. 68 *"the word of God may be likened…"* Bahá'u'lláh , Tablets of Bahá'u'lláh, 7.
    Lawḥ-i-Dunyá (Tablet of the World)
p. 69 *"Verily, I supplicate to God.."* 'Abdu'l-Bahá, Baha'I World Faith – Selected Writings of Baha'u'llah
    and 'Abdu'l-Baha ('Abdu'l-Baha's section only), Pages 361-362: gr4
p. 70 *"O Friends, consort with …"* 'Abdu'l-Bahá / A Traveler's Narrative
p. 71 *" O lord, unite and bind…"* 'Abdu'l-Bahá, The Promulgation of Universal Peace 82.
    All Souls Unitarian Church,
    " O My God! Unite the hearts.."
p. 72 *"O my God! O my God! Unite the Hearts…"* Bahá'u'lláh, Bahá'í Prayers: A Selection of
    Prayers Revealed by Bahá'u'lláh, the Báb, and 'Abdu'l-Bahá
p. 73 *"May the trees of your hearts…"* 'Abdu'l-Bahá , The Promulgation of Universal Peace 15. Studio Hall.
p. 74 *"O Son of Being!..."* Bahá'u'lláh, The Hidden Words, Part One: From the Arabic : Number 12
p. 75 *"Ye must become brilliant lamps…"* 'Abdu'l-Bahá, The Promulgation of Universal Peace, 109.
    Japanese Young Men's Christian Association
p. 76 *"**God is one**, the **effulgence** of **God is one**…"* 'Abdu'l-Bahá, The Promulgation of Universal Peace 121.
    Eighth Street Temple, Synagogue
p. 77 *"Be unto the world…"* 'Abdu'l-Bahá , Paris Talks 53, The last meeting
p. 78 *"True civilization will unfurl its banner …"* 'Abdu'l-Bahá / The Secret of Divine Civilization
p. 79 *"Open the doors of your hearts."* Bahá'u'lláh, **Tablets of Bahá'u'lláh,** 2. Lawḥ-i-Aqdas
    (The Most Holy Tablet)
p. 80 *"Use thy utmost power to sow and cast.."* 'Abdu'l-Bahá , Tablets of Abdul-Baha Abbas, Pages 171-172: gr4

p. 81 *"We ask God to endow…"* 'Abdu'l-Bahá , The Promulgation of Universal Peace, / 102. Coronation Hall
p. 82 *"The purpose of God in creating man…."* Bahá'u'lláh, **Gleanings from the Writings of Bahá'u'lláh** XXIX:
    "The purpose of God in creating man hath…"
p. 83 *"In **flower-spangled meadows…**"* 'Abdu'l-Bahá, **Selections from the Writings of 'Abdu'l-Bahá** 206:

"Praise be to Him Who hath rent the dark asunder,…"

p. 84 *"O friends! Be not careless…"* Bahá'u'lláh, Gleanings from the Writings of Baha'u'llah, XCVI: "The Pen of the Most High is unceasingly…"

p. 85 *"You must deal with all in loving-kindness…"* 'Abdu'l-Bahá, The Promulgation of Universal Peace, 3. Studio of Miss Phillips

p. 86 *"O Lord! Make this youth radiant…"* 'Abdu'l-Bahá, Bahá'í Prayers, A Selection of Prayers Revealed by Bahá'u'lláh, The Báb, and 'Abdu'l-Bahá" p. 37

p. 87 *"This is a new cycle of human power…"* 'Abdu'l-Bahá, `Abdu'l-Bahá in London, Pages 19-20: gr2

"The dispensation of Baha'u'llah.." Bahá'u'lláh, Tablets of Bahá'u'lláh, / Notes : Note 62

p. 88 *"The betterment of the world …"* Shoghi Effendi, The Advent of Divine Justice, Rectitude of Conduct

"Pure and holy deeds…." Bahá'u'lláh, The Hidden Words, Part Two: From the Persian : Number 69

"Let your acts be a guide…" Bahá'u'lláh, Gleanings From the Writings of Bahá'u'lláh, CXXXIX: "Let thine ear be attentive, O Nabíl-i-'A ẓam,…"

"Beautify your tongues…" Bahá'u'lláh, Gleanings From the Writings of Bahá'u'lláh, CXXXVI: "Say: Deliver your souls, O people, from…"

p. 89 *"O Son of Man! Rejoice in the gladness…".* Bahá'u'lláh, The Hidden Words, Part One: From the Arabic : Number 36

p. 90 *"Man must learn the lesson of kindness…"* 'Abdu'l-Bahá, **The Promulgation of Universal Peace**, 118. Universalist Church

p. 91 *"Shine out like the day-star…"* 'Abdu'l-Bahá, Selections From the Writings of 'Abdu'l-Bahá, 200**:** "O my spiritual loved ones! At a time when an …"

p. 92 *"Ye must therefore put forth…"* 'Abdu'l-Bahá, Selections From the Writings of `Abdu'l-Baha, Pages 140-141: fr1

p. 93 *"Work, for the day of ,…"* 'Abdu'l-Bahá, 'Abdu'l-Bahá in London, Pages 122-123: gr 2

p. 94 *"Verily, I pray God to make thy home…"*, 'Abdu'l-Bahá, Tablets of Abdul-Baha Abbas, p. 69.

p. 95 *"From the horizon of detachment.."* FIRE AND LIGHT (Compilation) Excerpts from the Bahá'í Sacred Writings… page 20. Compiled by Research Department of the Universal House of Justice. Hofheim-Langenhain: Baha'i Verlag, 1982

p. 96 *"The most important thing is to polish…"* 'Abdu'l-Bahá, The Promulgation of Universal Peace**.** 6. Union Meeting of Advanced Thought Centers

p. *97 "The instruction of these children…."* 'Abdu'l-Bahá, Selections from the Writings of 'Abdu'l-Bahá, 123: "O thou who gazest upon the Kingdom of God!…"

p. 98 *"The babe, like unto a tender…"* 'Abdu'l-Bahá, Tablets of Abdul-Baha Abbas, Pages 576-580: gr10

p. *99 "Say: God sufficeth ….."* The Báb, Selections from the Writings of the Báb. "Rid thou thyself of all attachments to aught except God, …"

p. 100 **"Strive, therefore, with heart and soul…"** 'Abdu'l-Bahá, Selections from the Writings of 'Abdu'l-Bahá**.**

p. 101 "We must now highly resolve to arise…." 'Abdu'l-Bahá , The Secret of Divine Civilization

Hello.
My name is Monika.
It is with excitement that I share with you this second collection of illustrations. It makes me very happy to have found a drawing project that may enable the beauty of the
Bahá'í Writings travel far and wide like seeds scattered by the wind.
My hope is that the artwork can provide a gentle bridge between the Holy Writings and the soul. whilst providing a means for creative inspiration. relaxation and happiness.

monikaseasand@gmail.com
WORD SPIRITS
Drawn in Yeppoon Qld, Australia 2015